# HARLEM
# HELLFIGHTERS

In memory of Aaron Frisch (1975–2013),
with our appreciation and gratitude. –JPL & GK

Text copyright © 2014 J. Patrick Lewis    Illustrations copyright © 2014 Gary Kelley
Designed by Rita Marshall with Gary Kelley
Published in 2014 by Creative Editions    P.O. Box 227, Mankato, MN 56002 USA
Creative Editions is an imprint of The Creative Company.
**Library of Congress Cataloging-in-Publication Data**
Harlem hellfighters / by J. Patrick Lewis; illustrated by Gary Kelley.
Summary: A regiment of African American soldiers from Harlem journeys across the Atlantic to fight alongside the
French in World War I, inspiring a continent with their brand of jazz music.    ISBN 978-1-56846-246-2
1. United States. Army. Infantry Regiment, 369th—Juvenile literature. 2. World War, 1914–1918—Participation, African
American—Juvenile literature. 3. United States. Army—African American troops—History—20th century—Juvenile
literature. 4. African American soldiers—History—20th century—Juvenile literature. 5. Harlem (New York, N.Y.)—
Biography—Juvenile literature. I. Kelley, Gary, illustrator. II. Title.
D570.33369th.L49 2014    940.54'03—dc23    2013041370
9 8 7 6 5 4 3 2

# HARLEM
# HELLFIGHTERS

## J. PATRICK LEWIS & GARY KELLEY

Creative Editions

# INTRODUCTION

Although World War I—the Great War—was global, it was fought "over there," on the European continent, from August 1914 through November 1918. Its horrific destruction is almost indescribable: Nine million soldiers and untold civilians died in what is the sixth deadliest conflict in history.

The United States was a latecomer. After two and a half years of remaining "neutral," the U.S. joined the battle in April 1917. An important chapter of America's involvement in the war is often minimized: the critical role of more than 350,000 black American soldiers.

One such unit, mobilized as the 15th New York National Guard, was federalized as the 369th Infantry Regiment. They became the Harlem Hellfighters, so named by the Germans for their tenacity. They also called themselves the Men of Bronze or the Black Rattlers, and they would make history not only on the battlefield but also for a wholly original musical creation, a mix of primitive jazz, blues, and upbeat ragtime never heard before.

Inspired by James "Big Jim" Reese Europe, the charismatic leader of this regimental band of brothers, the Hellfighters' musical sound was born of racial pride that "came from our souls." Big Jim's rousing instrumentals carried the beleaguered Hellfighters through France and 191 days under German siege, more than any other American regiment.

James Reese Europe's big band sound, as one general put it, was exactly what this war needed.

## RECRUITED IN SONG
### April 1916

America's late declaration of war against the Germans filled enlistment offices everywhere. In New York state, politicians enlisted magnetic bandleader James Europe to help assemble a new black regiment in Harlem.
And the cavalcade was on.

Even the tops of city buses hosted Big Jim's band, recruits hopping aboard to the irresistible tug of patriotism, ragtime, and jazz. Dismissed by much of white America as "darkies playing soldiers," porters, butlers, hotel doormen, elevator operators— 2,000 strong—volunteered for the cause.

## DRILLED DOWN SOUTH
### Summer 1917
### Spartanburg, South Carolina

Sent to train in a land unwelcome,
the 15th (Colored), as they were
first known, soon asked themselves
whether German bullets could be
as fatal as the rifle eyes of Southern
gentry, women—highborn or down-
and-out—triggered to rage, minis-
ters sold on buckshot salvation, and
deputy sheriffs certain that black
was not any color of the rainbow.

# ACROSS THE WORLD
## December 1917

The *Pocahontas,* a German-built troopship
seized in war, hauled away its cargo
of men and innocence.

in the mid-Atlantic
fog of history, two
dark ships passed
in the night . . .

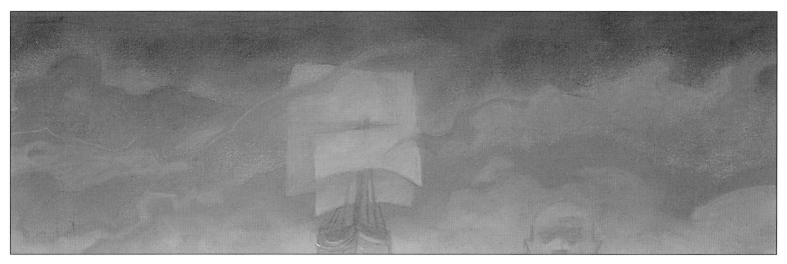

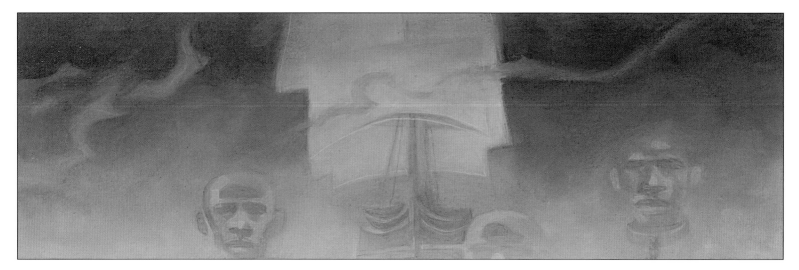

On a winter-savage sea, the specter of
enemy subs, lurking at fearful fathoms,
haunted the restless troops until the ship
was moored—three long weeks from
America—to the planet France.

Ranging all along the Brittany harbor wall,
frenzied Frenchmen swayed to Jim Europe's
pizzazz jazz "Marseillaise."

But the band finally packed up,
soon to be sent to a land
no poet could portray.

# ORDERS TO STAND
## 1918

The first three months belied all expectations.
Where were the marching orders to the front?
The American war machine rewarded the 369th
with the same third-rate jobs blacks faced at home:
grunt work.

They picked and shoveled dams, built hospitals in
mud, laid rail lines spiked in blood, and dredged the
port of Saint-Nazaire.

In the teeth of the raging cold, men waged a desperate campaign for morale by writing letters home.

## THAT HARLEM SOUND
### February 1918

Troop trains rattled across a nation bound up in fear and ice. One unforgettable mission sent Jim Europe's band high into the Alps, where it found fame that sent it over the top: the Village of the Baths (*Aix-les-Bains*).

In this elite playground, the band served honey through a horn to war-weary dough-boys on leave. Each night shimmered like Christmas Eve.

Who could transpose that rhythm to the page? Europe's big band "jazz spasm," riffing to ten pianos, turned listeners' bones to liquid—cymbal-cornet-clarinet clash coursing in the blood.

# ORDERS TO MOVE
## March–April 1918

"Chocolate soldiers"—"les enfants perdu"
(lost infants, or soldiers on perilous missions)—
finally caught the train to the Great War.

Before they fought the Huns, they were taught French
radios, maps, Lebel rifles, mortars, long bayonets, short
rations, delousing, homing pigeons, the real or ghostly
sounds of German shells . . .

Despite homesickness, fatigue, rats, and the
unknown, comrades-in-arms would confront the sput-
tering mortars and stuttering guns of the summer to
come with one response: *Vive la France!*

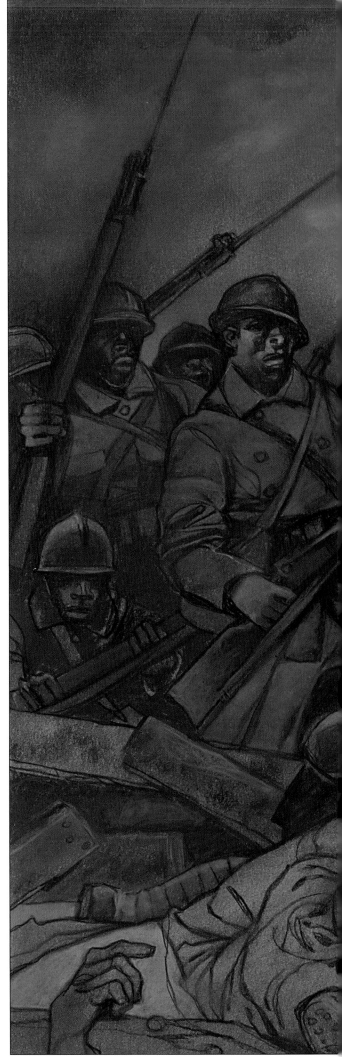

# "THE BATTLE OF HENRY JOHNSON"
## PORTRAIT OF AN ACCIDENTAL HERO
### May 1918

The Harlem Hellfighters defined courage,
none more than red cap Albany porter
Henry Johnson. Standing night sentry
in Hauzy Woods with Private Needham Roberts,
they were overrun by the enemy.

Gutted twenty-one times,
the five-foot-four-inch Johnson somehow
killed four, put 24 to rout with three bullets,
a handful of grenades, and a nine-inch bolo knife,
before saving the life of the seriously wounded
Roberts.

"Black Death" Johnson won the Croix de Guerre,
France's highest military honor, the first ever given
to an American serviceman, an African American
at that.

"One of the five bravest soldiers in the Great War,"
said Theodore Roosevelt.

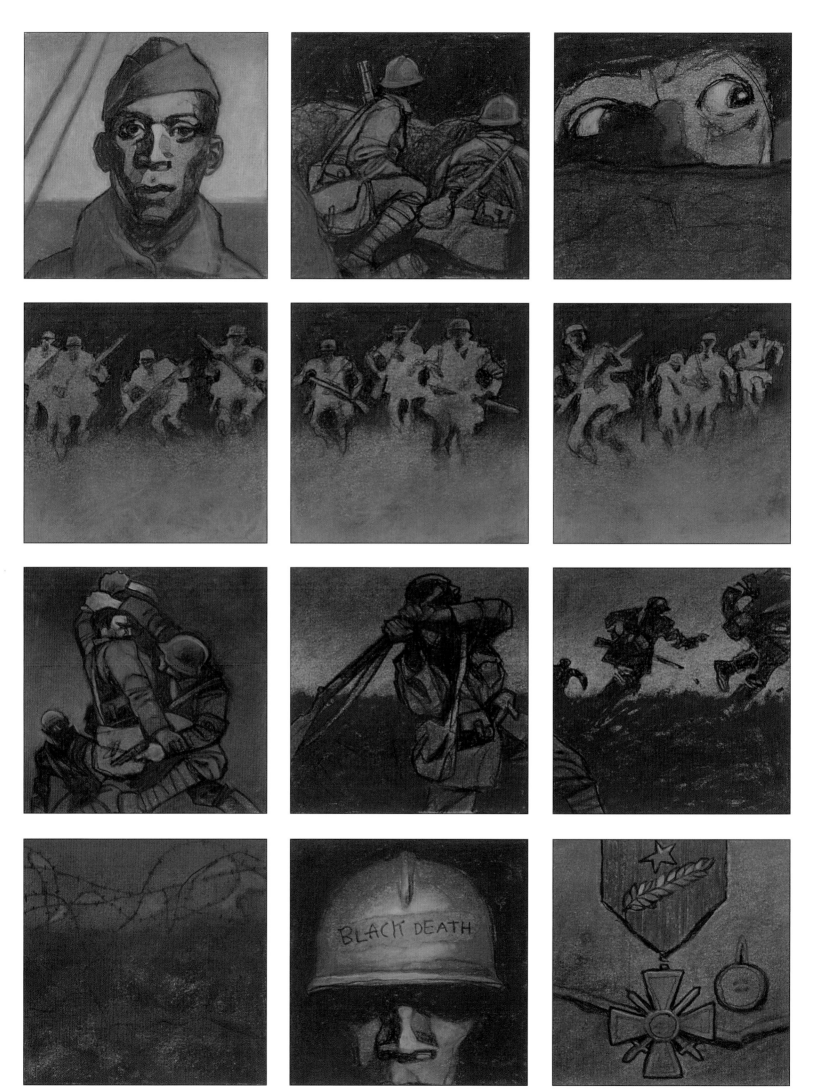

## BACK HOME

President Woodrow Wilson failed to stand against a rash of lynchings in the South until the headlines shamed his silence.

The Hellfighters were writing their own epigram: At war, men die bravely and escape the rope. At home, cowards lasso trees suspending hope.

## A BREAK FROM BATTLE
June 1918
Maffrecourt, France

Relieved from trench duty, Jim Europe found a modest farmhouse in a remote hamlet alive with birdsong. At a cob-webbed piano, he'd spend most of the day and half the night writing songs—"I'm an Observation Tower of My Own," "I've Got the Map of Your Heart"—pretending war was over there.

Later, while hospitalized after a gas attack, Jim wrote his best-known song, the breezy and lyrical "On Patrol in No Man's Land," whose refrain simulated the sounds of actual bombardment.

Across the Dormoise River,
bracing for a massive blitz,
the 369th heard only bird calls
in shadows.

The moon took cover
in a bunker of clouds.

When Fritz rose up, Frenchmen,
Yanks, and Germans toppled
like bowling pins onto a boneyard
riverbank. A third of the regiment
was either shrapnel-gashed
or pitched into unsung oblivion.

In the Sechault ruins,
buildings burned through the night,
much like German provocation
for fighting on. Still, both sides
knew the war was nearly over.

## THE TALLY

Mustered in: 2,000 Harlem Hellfighters.

Killed or wounded: 1,500 in 4 French campaigns.

Citations: the Croix de Guerre to 171 Hellfighters; the Medal of Honor to 1 officer (white).

Known as: "The regiment that never lost a man captured, a trench, or a foot of ground."

Jim Europe's band: 90 musicians on parade; 30–50 in ballroom orchestra.

## HAPPY HORNS
### Armistice Day
### November 11, 1918

The band jammed in Bitschwiller,
a village that never knew such sound.
Wide-eyed French citizens crazily
kissed each other, running door
to door to mourn, *Mon Dieu*,
the missing or to mark the end of war.
Townsfolk knocked back glasses
of liberation with free beer chasers,
and plugged into "The Memphis Blues."

## THE HOMECOMING
February 17, 1919
New York City

With the Mayor's blessing,
the Hellfighters marched up
Fifth Avenue to "All of No Man's
Land Is Ours," saluting the Allies'
victory over the Central Powers.
When the band lit up the afternoon
with "Here Comes My Daddy Now,"
grateful mothers hugged their sons,
wives kissed their husbands
in a Harlem rapture of tears
to flood the East River.

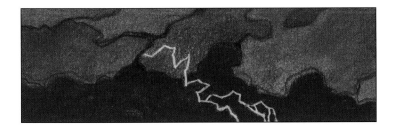

## GOODBYE, JIM
### May 9, 1919
### Boston, Massachusetts

Wind and rain screamed off the bay.
Lightning daggered the land the night
Jim Europe planned to make floors rumble
and ceilings pop at Mechanics Hall.

But Herbert Wright, a mad drummer
with a tripwire temper, drew a blade
when Jim had merely "frowned" at him.
Herbert nicked the bandleader's neck.

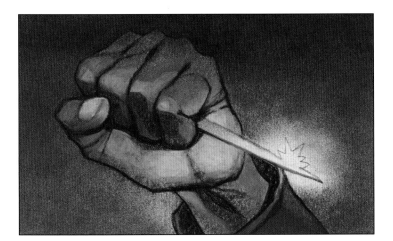

The "flesh wound" severed the jugular
of this giant of invincibility, laid waste
by folly and the outrageous powers
of circumstance.

The chaplain's bowed head told the story:
James Reese Europe's unique sound,
cut short at thirty-nine by a penknife.

## IN MEMORIAM
May 10, 1919
Boston, Massachusetts

Governor Calvin Coolidge stood
at Robert Gould Shaw's Memorial,
the jewel of the neighborhood.
Fifty-six years after Shaw's 54th
Massachusetts Regiment had fought
as freed slaves for the Union,
the Hellfighters' band, honoring
their forebears, performed as called upon.
But the wreath intended for Shaw's
Civil War monument would grace
instead Jim Europe's rose-wrapped casket.

## THE JAZZ KING OF BROADWAY
May 13, 1919
New York City

Three days later,
the first black man ever to be given
a public funeral in the city of New York
rolled through the streets of Harlem
past a delirium of mourners.

In black armbands, the Hellfighters
marched last, their hushed instruments
at their sides.

# BIBLIOGRAPHY

Badger, Reid. *A Life in Ragtime: A Biography of James Reese Europe*. New York: Oxford University Press, 1995.

Barbeau, Arthur E., and Florette Henri. *The Unknown Soldiers: African-American Troops in WWI*. New York: Da Capo Press, 1996.

Europe, James Reese. *Lieut. Jim Europe's 369th "Hell Fighters" Band: The Complete Recordings*. Memphis Archives 7020, 1996, compact disc. Recorded March–May 1919.

Harris, Bill. *The Hellfighters of Harlem: African-American Soldiers Who Fought for the Right to Fight for Their Country*. New York: Carroll & Graf, 2002.

Harris, Stephen L. *Harlem's Hell Fighters: The African-American 369th Infantry in World War I*. Washington, D.C.: Brassey's, 2003.

Little, Arthur W. *From Harlem to the Rhine: The Story of New York's Colored Volunteers*. New York: Haskell House, 1974.

Myers, Walter Dean, and William Miles. *The Harlem Hellfighters: When Pride Met Courage*. New York: HarperCollins, 2006.

Nelson, Peter N. *A More Unbending Battle: The Harlem Hellfighters' Struggle for Freedom in WWI and Equality at Home*. New York: Basic Civitas, 2009.

# ARTIST'S NOTES

page 6: American illustrator James Montgomery Flagg's iconic watercolor image of "Uncle Sam" inspired this "I Want You" poster image. More than 4 million copies of Flagg's poster were printed between 1917 and 1918.

pages 18–19: French artist Eugene Delacroix commemorated the July Revolution of 1830 in his painting *Liberty Leading the People* (1830), whose main figure is itself reminiscent of the spirit of the 1789 French Revolution.

page 23: Referencing a number of French Impressionist works—most notably Claude Monet's *Poppies, near Argenteuil* (1873)—this landscape evokes the peacefulness of a pre-war French countryside.

page 26: The lively scenario pictured in the bottom right-hand corner is informed by French Impressionist Pierre-Auguste Renoir's *Dance at Bougival* (1883), which features a couple whirling to a tune at an open-air cafe.

page 29: The bronze monument depicted at the top of this page was completed in 1897 by American sculptor Augustus Saint-Gaudens. The Latin inscription can be translated as "He gave up everything to serve the republic."